Learn to **KNIT** on
LONG LOOMS™

Designs by Anne Bipes

HOUSE of
WHITE
BIRCHES

PUBLISHERS
SINCE 1947

Table of Contents

Reversible Checkerboard Afghan, *page 26*

14 Mocha Latte Scarf

16 Magic Mobius Scarf

18 Color Block for Baby

21 Crystal Blues Scarf

22 Pixie Hat & Scarf for Dolly & Me

25 Woodsy-Warmth Shawl

26 Reversible Checkerboard Afghan

28 Garden Party Set

32 Beaded Beauty Set

37 Arrowhead Double-Knit Scarf

42 Earth Mother's Slippers

44 Toasty-Toes Moccasins

Arrowhead Double-Knit Scarf, *page 37*

Pixie Hat & Scarf for Dolly & Me, *page 22*

Woodsy-Warmth Shawl, *page 25*

General Information

Terminology

Anchor peg: The small peg at the end of the loom that is at a 90-degree angle to the loom. The beginning tail of the yarn is tied to this peg to hold it while the first several rows are being knit. After that, the beginning tail can be removed from the anchor peg.

Bind Off: Removing the knitting from the loom by finishing and securing each stitch in the row.

Cast On: The first wrap of the loom to put a single loop of yarn onto each peg.

Knit Off: Generally, a knit stitch is made by bringing the bottom loop on the peg up and over the top loop and 0off the peg toward the center of the loom. Sometimes, a knit stitch is made by bringing the bottom loop over two or more top loops, or by bringing two or more bottom loops over the top loop.

Peg pairs: Two parallel pegs equidistant from the anchor peg.

Remove Knitting From the Loom: Taking the knitting off the loom, leaving a row of live stitches that have a strand of scrap yarn running through them.

Scrap Yarn: A piece of yarn that is not part of the project itself, but is used to hold live stitches temporarily. It is best if the scrap yarn is a different color than the project color, smooth in texture and a larger diameter than the project yarn.

Tail: The cut end of yarn not part of the knitting. The beginning tail is the first 6 inches or so before the yarn is used to cast on or continue the knitting. The ending tail is the last 6 inches or so after the last stitch or bind off.

Wrap the Loom: To put the yarn on the pegs in a certain order until all pegs have a new loop on them. For some stitch patterns, all pegs are wrapped in one pass of the loom. For others, the yarn goes from top to bottom back to the top again before all pegs are wrapped.

Cast On

Make a slip knot about 5 inches from the end of the yarn and put it on an anchor peg at one end of the loom.

Wrap the yarn around the outside of the pegs on the loom, first peg on the left, second peg on the right, third peg on the left, fourth peg on the right, etc., for as many peg pairs as the pattern indicates.

Bring the yarn straight across to the other side of the loom.

Continue wrapping in a "Z" pattern back to the beginning, using the pegs that are not yet wrapped.

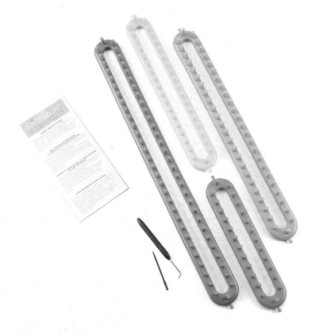

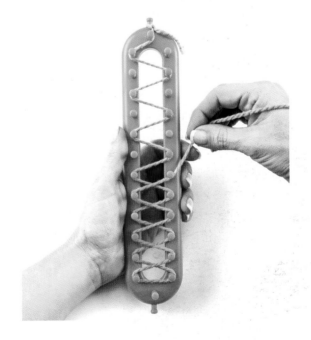

House of White Birches, Berne, Indiana 46711 AnniesAttic.com

Lay a piece of scrap yarn over the wrapped yarn. Let the tails of the scrap yarn hang between the wrapped yarn and the loom. The scrap yarn tails can be tied together so it stays in place.

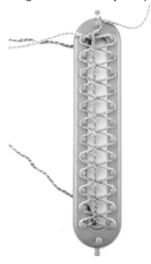

Push the wraps down on the pegs so there is space to put another wrap of yarn above them on the pegs. Unless otherwise specified, each yarn wrap goes above the existing wrap on the pegs.

The cast on is complete. The next wrap of the loom is the first row, in the stitch pattern indicated in the project instructions.

Finishing the Cast-On Edge

Start at the edge of the knitting opposite the beginning tail. Untie the scrap yarn.

Put a slip knot loosely on a crochet hook.

Insert the crochet hook into the first loop on the scrap yarn.

Wrap the working yarn around the crochet hook, and pull it through the two loops on the hook.

There will be one loop left on the crochet hook.

Insert the crochet hook into the next two loops on the scrap yarn—they cross over each other. Wrap the working yarn around the crochet hook and pull it through the three loops on the hook, leaving one loop left on the hook.

Continue across the width of the knitting.

The last stitch is made with the single loop left on the scrap yarn.

Cut the working yarn, leaving a 6-inch tail. Make one more crochet stitch. Then, wrap the crochet hook with both the working yarn and the beginning tail, pulling them both all the way through the loop on the hook. Pull gently on the working yarn tail to close the loop against the knitting.

Gently pull the scrap yarn free from the knitting.

Bind Off

With the working yarn on the right end of the loom, bring the loops from the far side of the loom to the near side.

The loom will have no loops on one side and two loops on the other side.

Bring the working yarn to the left in front of the first two pegs, and knit them off, bringing the two bottom loops over the top one loop.

Make sure the new loops are loose.

Take the second loop off the loom and put it on the first peg. Knit off the first peg.

Move the remaining loop to the empty peg on the left.

Knit the next peg as before, and then move it above the loop on the peg to the right. Knit off. Move the remaining loop to the empty peg on the left.

Continue across the width of the knitting.

When there is one loop left on the loom cut the yarn, leaving a 6-inch tail. Wrap the peg and knit off. Wrap the peg again and knit off, pulling the cut yarn end through the loop. Remove the loop from the loom and gently pull the tail to close the loop against the knitting.

Remove Knitting From Loom

With the working yarn on the right end of the loom, bring the loops from the far side of the loom to the near side.

The loom will have no loops on one side and two loops on the other side.

Cut a piece of scrap yarn 2–3 times longer than the width of the knitting and thread it into a blunt tapestry needle.

Starting at one end of the loom, bring the needle through the first loop on the peg, sliding the needle along the groove in the peg from the bottom to the top.

Thread the needle through each peg on the loom in order, sliding the needle along the groove in the peg from the bottom to the top.

House of White Birches, Berne, Indiana 46711   AnniesAttic.com

When all loops have been threaded, remove the loops from the pegs.

Tie the ends of the scrap yarn together to secure them so the loops remain captured. Leave enough slack in the scrap yarn so the knitting isn't gathered.

Add a New Skein/Change Color

A new strand of yarn can be added at any point in the row, though color changes generally happen on the last stitch of the row.

Cut the old color yarn, leaving a 6-inch tail. Wrap the last peg with the old color and the new color yarn above it. Knit off to secure both yarn ends.

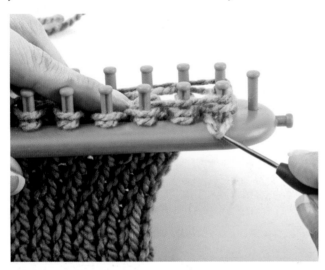

Continue knitting in your stitch pattern with just the new color.

The yarn tails can be laid across the knitting in between the pegs to hide them so they don't need to be woven in later.

Invisible Stitch Join

Lay the two pieces of knit fabric side by side. Thread an 18-inch length of yarn in a blunt tapestry needle.

You will be catching the yarn where it crisscrosses between the upper and lower edges of the fabric.

Starting at the bottom edges of the knit pieces, put the needle in the first crisscross on the fabric on the right.

Put the needle in the first two crisscrosses on the fabric on the left.

Catch the next two crisscrosses on the right-hand fabric.

Continue in this manner, catching two crisscrosses on each side.

Every couple inches, hold the beginning yarn tail and pull gently on the yarn near the last stitch. This will straighten the stitches, making them almost straight up and down instead of right and left, and will draw the two knit pieces close together, hiding the seam.

Crochet Slip-Stitch Join

Make a slip knot and put it on the crochet hook.

With wrong sides together, match the edges of the two knit pieces so the edge stitches line up.

Put the crochet hook into the top edge loop of each knit piece.

Wrap the yarn around the crochet hook and pull it through the three loops on the hook, leaving one new loop on the crochet hook.

Repeat the last two steps until the end of the seam is reached. With one loop on the crochet hook, wrap the yarn around the hook and pull it through the loop. Wrap and pull through again. Cut the yarn, leaving a 6-inch tail. Pull on the loop until the cut edge comes through. Gently pull on the tail until the loop closes snug against the knitting.

Weave in tails.

Decrease

The decrease is done using the three peg pairs at the end of the loom.

Move the loops on pegs 2 to pegs 3.

Move the loops on pegs 1 to pegs 2.

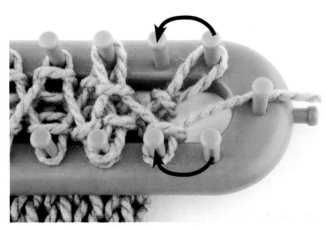

Pegs 1 are empty, there is one loop on each of pegs 2, and there are two loops on each of pegs 3.

When knitting the next row, pegs 3 are knit off as two-over-one.

Increase & Moving Knit-Off Loops

The increase is done using three peg pairs.

Move the loops on pegs 1 away from the knitting by one peg.

Move the next set of loops to the empty pegs.

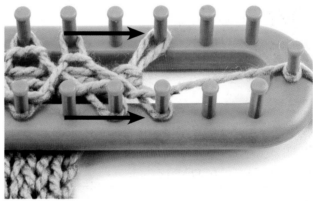

Move the just-knit-off loops from the back sides of the pegs on either side of the empty peg to the empty peg.

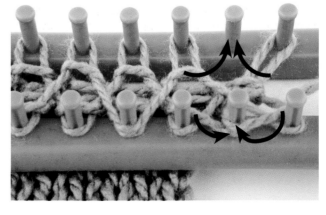

This prevents a hole in the fabric at the increase point.

Wrap and knit the next row. When knitting the peg containing the just-knit-off loops, bring the bottom two loops over the one top loop.

Knit Off

When there are two loops on the peg, insert the hook tool into the bottom loop. Pull it away from the loom slightly, and then bring it up over the top loop and off the peg. Place the loop behind the peg in the center of the loom.

In some cases, there will be more than two loops on the peg. Follow the pattern instructions for knitting off two-over-one (two bottom loops over one top loop), one-over-two (one bottom loop over two top loops), etc. ❖

Tips for Success

- When binding off and finishing the cast-on end, make sure your stitches are large enough that the ends can stretch with the knitting instead of constricting it. Check the stretch before cutting the working yarn, in case you need to redo the stitches to make them looser.

- When choosing scrap strands for the cast on and removing the knitting from the loom, select yarn that is smooth, not textured, in a contrasting color, and in a similar or larger thickness than the working yarn. This will make it easier to see and crochet the stitches when finishing the ends.

- After wrapping the loom for a row of stitches, knit off the last peg you wrapped first. This will anchor the yarn so it doesn't come loose from the loom.

Stitching Instructions

Stockinette

This wrap is the same as the cast-on wrap. You will wrap the yarn in both directions to complete one row.

Wrap the yarn around the outside pegs of the loom, first peg on the left, second peg on the right, third peg on the left, fourth peg on the right, etc., for as many peg pairs as the pattern indicates. Make sure the yarn you are wrapping is closer to the top of the pegs than the loops that are already on the pegs.

Bring the yarn straight across to the other side of the loom.

Continue wrapping in a "Z" pattern back to the beginning, using the pegs that are not yet wrapped.

To knit off, bring the bottom loop over the top loop and off the peg toward the center of the loom. Knit off the last peg you wrapped first, to anchor the end of the yarn.

Double Stockinette

Wrap the loom as for the stockinette stitch.

Wrap the loom again, so there are three loops on each peg.

To knit off, bring the bottom loop over the top two loops and off the peg toward the center of the loom. Knit off the last peg you wrapped first, to anchor the end of the yarn.

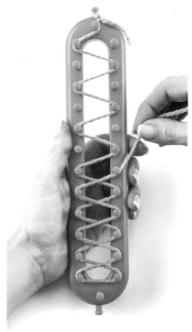

For the next row, wrap the loom once and knit off two-over-one.

To end the double stockinette stitch, knit off one row without wrapping the loom. This will leave one loop on each peg.

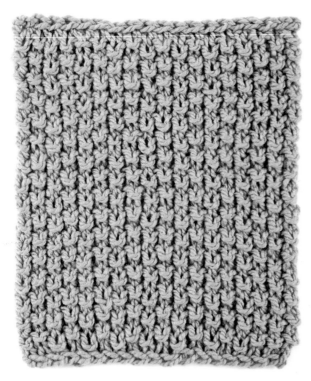

Purl

Wrap the loom as for the stockinette stitch, *except* put the working yarn below the existing loop on each peg.

Hold the hook tool so the hook is pointing downward.

Slide it in the groove on the peg behind the old loop.

Twist the tool slightly so the tip of the hook points away from the peg.

Slide the tool down a little so the end of the hook tool covers the new loop.

Twist the tool so the point scrapes in the groove until the tip points up; the bottom yarn loop will be captured by the hook.

Move the tool upwards above the loom, keeping the new loop captured.

Place the new loop back on the peg.

Continue with the remaining pegs to be purled.

Note: *Some patterns direct you to purl only one side of the knitting; the other side is knit as for the stockinette stitch.*

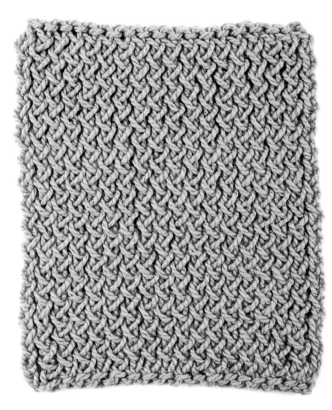

To knit off, bring the bottom loop over the top loop and off the peg toward the center of the loom. Knit off the last peg you wrapped first, to anchor the end of the yarn.

To start wrapping in the opposite direction, wrap the first peg pair first. When moving to the next peg pair, the working yarn will cross over the strand of yarn from the previous row, forming an "X" in the center of the loom. The yarn will not be tracing the wrap of the previous row.

Twisted Stockinette

This is a looser stitch than the stockinette stitch. You will wrap the yarn in one direction only on the loom to complete one row.

Bring the yarn between the first and second pegs on the left side of the loom. Wrap the yarn around the first peg in a clockwise direction until the yarn is in the center of the loom. Then bring the yarn between the first and second pegs on the right side of the loom. Wrap the yarn around the first peg in a counterclockwise direction until the yarn is in the center of the loom.

Bring the yarn between the second and third pegs on the left side of the loom, wrap in a clockwise direction, and bring it between the second and third pegs on the right side of the loom and wrap in a counterclockwise direction.

Continue in this manner until all peg pairs are wrapped.

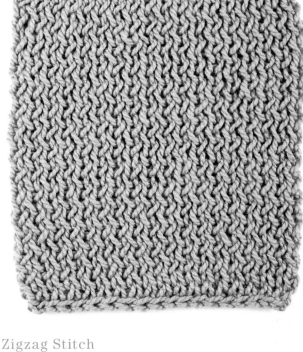

Zigzag Stitch

You will wrap the yarn in one direction only on the loom to complete one row.

Wrap the yarn around the first peg on the left side of the loom, and then around the first peg on the right side of the loom.

House of White Birches, Berne, Indiana 46711   AnniesAttic.com

Wrap the yarn around the second peg on the left side of the loom, and then around the second peg on the right side of the loom.

Continue in this manner until all peg pairs are wrapped.

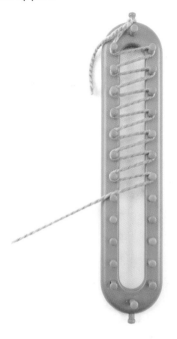

To knit off, bring the bottom loop over the top loop and off the peg toward the center of the loom. Knit off the last peg you wrapped first, to anchor the end of the yarn.

To start wrapping in the opposite direction, wrap the first peg pair first. When moving to the next peg pair, the working yarn will cross over the strand of yarn from the previous row, forming an "X" in the center of the loom. The yarn will not be tracing the wrap of the previous row.

Duplicate Zigzag Stitch

This stitch has a lot of sideways stretch. You will wrap the yarn in one direction only on the loom to complete one row.

Wrap the yarn around the first peg on the left side of the loom, and then around the first peg on the right side of the loom.

Wrap the yarn around the second peg on the left side of the loom, and then around the second peg on the right side of the loom.

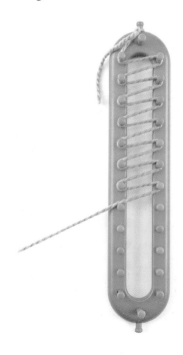

Continue in this manner until all peg pairs are wrapped.

To knit off, bring the bottom loop over the top loop and off the peg toward the center of the loom. Knit off the last peg you wrapped first, to anchor the end of the yarn.

To start wrapping in the opposite direction, wrap only one peg of the first peg pair. When moving to the next peg pair, the working yarn will trace the strand of yarn from the previous row. The yarn will not form an "X" in the center of the loom.

Wrap color A around the first left peg and Color B around the first right peg.

Hold one color in each hand. Pass the yarn strands to the other hand, then back again so the yarns are twisted around each other.

Wrap Color A around the second left peg and Color B around the second right peg.

Continue in this manner until all the pegs are wrapped. Keep the yarn crossovers as close to the center of the loom as possible to lessen the color bleed over on the outside of the knitting.

To knit off, bring the bottom loop over the top loop and off the peg toward the center of the loom. Knit off the last pegs you wrapped first, to anchor the ends of the yarn.

To start wrapping in the opposite direction, twist the two yarn colors before wrapping the first peg pair. ❖

Two-Color Stitch

This stitch looks like the stockinette stitch, with each side of the knitting a different color. Each color stays on either the right or left side of the loom, and the yarn strands twist around each other in the center. You will wrap the yarn in one direction only on the loom to complete one row.

Cast on with Color A. Make a slip knot with Color B and put it on the anchor peg.

Mocha Latte Scarf

Design by Anne Bipes

Skill Level
◼◻◻◻ BEGINNER

Finished Size
5 x 58 inches

Materials
- Red Heart Soft Yarn (worsted weight; 100% acrylic; 256 yds/140g per skein): 1 skein toast #1882
- 20-inch length scrap yarn
- Double-rake loom with at least 12 peg pairs
- Hook tool
- Size H/8 (5mm) crochet hook
- Scissors
- Tapestry needle

Gauge
9 stitches and 13 rows = 4 inches/10cm in Duplicate Zigzag stitch.

Exact gauge is not critical to this project.

Scarf
Cast on 12 peg pairs, lay scrap yarn.

Knit in duplicate zigzag stitch until scarf measures 58 inches or desired length.

Bind off.

Finish cast-on edge. Remove scrap yarn.

Weave in tails.

Make 6 tassels and attach to corners and center of each end of the scarf. ❖

Magic Mobius Scarf

Design by Anne Bipes

Skill Level

 BEGINNER

Finished Size
5 x 58 inches, before twisting

Materials
- Red Heart Soft Yarn (worsted weight; 100% acrylic; 256 yds/140g per skein): 1 skein mid blue #9820
- 20-inch length of scrap yarn

- Double-rake loom with at least 12 peg pairs
- Hook tool
- Size H/8 (5mm) crochet hook
- Scissors
- Tapestry needle

Gauge
9 stitches and 12 rows = 4 inches/10cm Zigzag stitch.

Exact gauge is not critical to this project.

Pattern Note
Scarf is worn wrapped around the neck twice, like two necklaces.

Scarf
Cast on 12 peg pairs, lay scrap yarn.

Knit in zigzag stitch until scarf measures 58 inches long or desired length.

Bind off.

Finish cast-on edge. Remove scrap yarn.

Weave in tails.

Finishing
Lay scarf flat and flip one end over once. Sew cast-on and bound-off edges together with a whipstitch. ❖

Panel 4

With Color D, cast on 23 peg pairs. Lay scrap yarn.

Knit 20 rows in stockinette stitch.

Change to Color A and knit 20 rows.

Change to Color C and knit 20 rows.

Change to Color B and knit 20 rows.

Change to Color F and knit 20 rows.

Change to Color E and knit 20 rows. Bind off. Finish cast-on edge. Remove scrap yarn. Weave in tails.

Panel 5

With Color B, cast on 23 peg pairs. Lay scrap yarn.

Knit 20 rows in stockinette stitch.

Change to Color E and knit 20 rows.

Change to Color F and knit 20 rows.

Change to Color A and knit 20 rows.

Change to Color D and knit 20 rows.

Change to Color C and knit 20 rows. Bind off. Finish cast-on edge. Remove scrap yarn. Weave in tails.

With Invisible stitch, join panels following chart. ❖

Crystal Blues Scarf

Design by Anne Bipes

Skill Level

■□□□ BEGINNER

Size

5 x 58 inches

Materials

- Red Heart Collage (worsted weight; 100% acrylic; 218 yds/100g per skein): 1 skein blue wave #2350
- 20-inch length of scrap yarn
- Double-rake loom with at least 12 peg pairs
- Hook tool
- Size H/8 (5mm) crochet hook
- Scissors
- Tapestry needle

Gauge

9 stitches and 12 rows = 4 inches/ 10cm in Twisted stockinette stitch.

Exact gauge is not critical to project.

Instructions

Cast on 12 peg pairs, lay scrap yarn.

Knit in twisted stockinette stitch until scarf measures 58 inches long or desired length.

Bind off.

Finish cast-on edge. Remove scrap yarn.

Weave in tails. ❖

Pixie Hat & Scarf for Dolly & Me

Designs by Anne Bipes

Skill Level
 EASY

Sizes
18-inch doll (toddler)

Instructions given fit smaller size, with larger size in parentheses. When only 1 number is given, it applies to both sizes.

Materials
- Lion Brand Jiffy (chunky weight; 100% acrylic; solids: 135 yds/85g; multis: 115 yds/70g per ball): 2 balls apple green #132, (rose spray #401)
- Lion Brand Fun Fur (chunky weight; 100% polyester; 57 yds/40g per ball): 2 balls confetti #206
- Two 20-inch lengths of scrap yarn
- Double-rake loom with at least 24 (30) peg pairs
- Hook tool
- Size H/8 (5mm) crochet hook
- Scissors
- Tapestry needle
- Soft brush

Gauge
10 stitches and 13 rows = 4 inches/10cm in Stockinette stitch.

Exact gauge is not critical to project.

Pattern Note
When incorporating the fur yarn, wrap only the pegs used for the hat portion, not the entire loom. Do not cut the yarn, just let it drop until you pick it up on the next row.

Instructions
Cut a 53- (70-) inch piece of the chunky yarn, set aside.

At one end of the loom, with chunky yarn cast on 8 (10) pegs, lay scrap yarn.

Knit 50 (75) rows in stockinette stitch.

Wrap 24 (30) pegs. Lay scrap yarn for the new pegs. Knit off pegs with two loops.

Wrap loom again, adding in 2 strands of fur yarn, starting and ending at pegs 8 (10) and knit off. Repeat 6 more times. Cut fur yarn.

Wrap loom again, incorporating fur tail into hat portion and knit off.

Knit 19 (39) rows.

Wrap loom, adding in 2 strands of fur yarn beginning and ending at pegs 8 (10) and knit off. Repeat 6 more times. Cut fur yarn.

Bring loops on pegs 9 (11)–24 (30) to one side of the loom to prepare for bind off.

With reserved strand of yarn, make a slip knot and put it on the crochet hook. Put two loops from peg 24 (30) onto the crochet hook. Wrap the yarn on the crochet hook and pull through the three loops (crochet slip stitch). Continue in this manner to peg 9 (11). Put the single remaining loop on the crochet hook onto peg 8 (10).

Knit 50 (75) rows using pegs 1–8 (10).

Bring loops to one side of the loom and bind off.

Finish cast-on edge. Remove scrap yarn.

Weave in tails.

Finishing

Fold hat portion so the two bands of fur yarn are overlapping. Beginning at fur edge on the outside of the hat, close the top seam with a crochet slip stitch. Bring tails to the inside of the hat and weave in. Brush the fur yarn with a soft brush to bring the ends of the fur strands to the outside of the knitting. ❖

Woodsy-Warmth Shawl

Design by Anne Bipes

Skill Level
■□□□ BEGINNER

Finished Size
11 x 58 inches

Materials

- Red Heart Collage (worsted weight; 100% acrylic; 218 yds/100g per skein): 3 skeins landscape green #2629
- 30-inch length of scrap yarn
- Double-rake loom with at least 30 peg pairs
- Hook tool
- Size H/8 (5mm) crochet hook
- Scissors
- Tapestry needle

Gauge
12 stitches and 14 rows = 4 inches/10cm in Stockinette stitch.

Exact gauge is not critical to this project.

Shawl
Cast on 30 peg pairs, lay scrap yarn.

Knit in stockinette stitch until shawl measures 58 inches long or desired length.

Bind off.

continued on page 46

House of White Birches, Berne, Indiana 46711

Reversible Checkerboard Afghan

Design by Anne Bipes

Skill Level
 EASY

Finished Size
50 x 68 inches

Materials
- Red Heart Soft Yarn (worsted weight; 100% acrylic; 256 yds/140g per skein): 6 skeins cherry red #5142 (A)
- Red Heart Collage (worsted weight; 100% acrylic; 218 yds/100g per skein): 6 skeins ice storm #2407 (B)
- 36-inch lengths of scrap yarn: 8
- Double-rake loom with at least 30 peg pairs
- Hook tool
- Size H/8 (5mm) crochet hook
- Scissors
- Tapestry needle

Gauge
10 stitches and 16 rows = 4 inches/10cm in Stockinette stitch.

Exact gauge is not critical to project.

Pattern Note
Be sure the yarn colors start on the same side of the loom on each panel.

Instructions

Panel
Make 4

Cast on 30 pegs with B, lay scrap yarn.

Step 1: With both colors, use 2-Color wrap technique to wrap 5 pegs, and then switch colors every 5 pegs for 6 sets of 5.

Step 2: Knit 8 rows.

Step 3: Wrap the next row, switching colors to the opposite side of the loom.

Step 4: Knit 8 rows.

Repeat Steps 1–4 until 28 blocks (224 rows) are complete.

Cut A yarn, leaving a 6-inch tail.

Wrap the loom with B as for the stockinette stitch and knit off. Cut yarn, leaving a 6-inch tail.

Bring loops from one side of the loom to the pegs on the other side.

Thread scrap yarn into a tapestry needle, thread through loops and remove the knitting from the loom.

Finishing
With B, use the Invisible stitch to attach the 4 panels, matching cast-on and bound-off edges and maintaining the checkerboard pattern.

With B, finish cast-on and bound-off edges, working from one side of the afghan to the other. Remove scrap yarn. Weave in tails. ❖

Garden Party Set

Design by Anne Bipes

- Double-rake loom with at least 9 (18) peg pairs
- Hook tool
- Size H/8 (5mm) crochet hook
- Scissors
- Tapestry needle

Gauge

10 stitches and 23 rows = 4 inches/10cm in Double stockinette stitch.

Exact gauge is not critical to project.

Instructions

Cast on 9 (18) peg pairs. Lay scrap yarn.

Wrap loom 2 more times. Knit off, bringing bottom loop over the upper two loops.

Knit 13 (34) more rows.

Without wrapping loom again, knit off by bringing the bottom loop over the top loop and off the peg. One loop will be left on each peg.

Bring loops from one side of the loom to the other and bind off.

Finish cast-on edge. Remove scrap yarn.

Weave in tails.

Trivet and Four Coasters

Skill Level

 BEGINNER

Finished Sizes

Coasters: 3½ inches square
Trivet: 7 inches square

Instructions are given for coasters, with trivet in parentheses. When only 1 number is given, it applies to both pieces.

Materials

- Pisgah Yarn & Dyeing Co. Peaches & Creme (worsted weight; 100% cotton; 98 yds/2 oz per ball): 1 ball desert bloom #188
- 20- (25-) inch length of scrap yarn

Place Mat

Skill Level
 EASY

Finished Size
12 x 18 inches

Materials
- Pisgah Yarn & Dyeing Co. Peaches & Creme (worsted weight; 100% cotton; 98 yds/2 oz per ball): 3 balls desert bloom #188 (makes 1 place mat)
- 36-inch length of scrap yarn
- Double-rake loom with at least 30 peg pairs
- Hook tool
- Size H/8 (5mm) crochet hook
- Scissors
- Tapestry needle

Gauge
10 stitches and 23 rows = 4 inches/10cm in Double stockinette stitch.

Exact gauge is not critical to this project.

Pattern Stitches

Pattern A

Row 1: Knit off pegs 5 and 7 by bringing the bottom loop over the top loop and off the loom, leaving just one loop on each peg. Move remaining loops 5 to pegs 4 and loops 7 to pegs 6.

Row 2: Knit off pegs 24 and 26 by bringing the bottom loop over the top loop and off the loom, leaving just one loop on each peg. Move remaining loops 26 to pegs 27 and loops 24 to pegs 25.

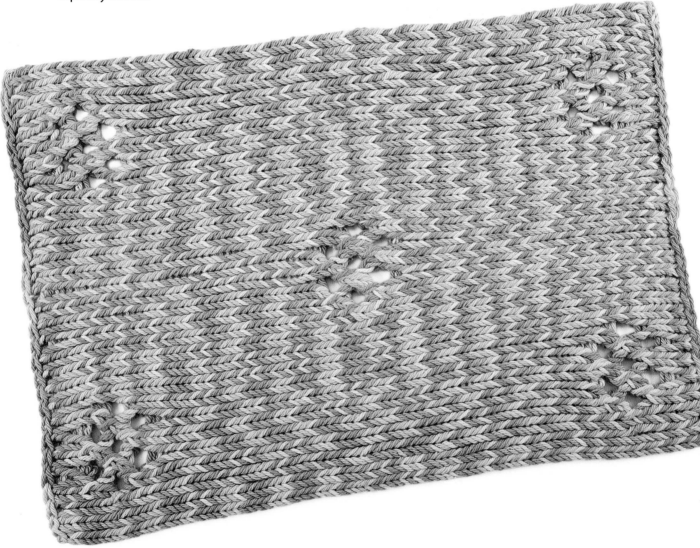

Row 3: Wrap loom, including empty pegs and knit off all pegs with three or more loops. (Only pegs 5, 7, 24 and 26 will not be knit off.)

Row 4: Repeat Row 3.

Pattern B

Row 1: Knit off pegs 4, 6 and 8 by bringing the bottom loop over the top loop and off the loom, leaving just one loop on each peg. Move remaining loops 4 to pegs 3, loops 6 to pegs 5 and loops 8 to pegs 7.

Row 2: Knit off pegs 23, 25 and 27 by bringing the bottom loop over the top loop and off the loom, leaving just one loop on each peg. Move remaining loops 27 to pegs 28, loops 25 to pegs 26 and loops 23 to pegs 24.

Row 3: Wrap loom, including empty pegs, and knit off all pegs with three or more loops. (Only pegs 4, 6, 8, 23, 25 and 27 will not be knit off.)

Row 4: Repeat Row 3.

Pattern C

Row 1: Knit off pegs 14 and 16 by bringing the bottom loop over the top loop and off the loom, leaving just one loop on each peg. Move remaining loops 14 to pegs 15 and loops 16 to pegs 17.

Row 2: Wrap loom, including empty pegs and knit off all pegs with three or more loops. (Only pegs 14 and 16 will not be knit off.)

Row 3: Repeat Row 2.

Pattern D

Row 1: Knit off pegs 13, 15 and 17 by bringing the bottom loop over the top loop and off the loom, leaving just one loop on each peg. Move remaining loops 13 to pegs 14, loops 15 to pegs 16 and loops 17 to pegs 18.

Row 2: Wrap loom, including empty pegs and knit off all pegs with three or more loops. (Only pegs 13, 15 and 17 will not be knit off.)

Row 3: Repeat Row 2.

Instructions

Cast on 30 peg pairs, lay scrap yarn.

Wrap loom 2 more times. Knit off, bringing bottom one loop over the upper two loops.

Knit 4 rows.

Follow Pattern A.

Knit 2 rows.

Follow Pattern B.

Knit 2 rows.

Follow Pattern A.

Knit 29 rows.

Follow Pattern C.

Knit 2 rows.

Follow Pattern D.

Knit 2 rows.

Follow Pattern C.

Knit 29 rows.

Follow Pattern A.

Knit 2 rows.

Follow Pattern B.

Knit 2 rows.

Follow Pattern A.

Knit 4 rows.

Without wrapping loom again, knit off by bringing the bottom loop over the top loop and off the peg. One loop will be left on each peg.

Bring loops from one side of the loom to the other and bind off.

Finish cast-on edge. Remove scrap yarn.

Weave in tails.

Finishing

Block place mat by pinning to a towel. Spray with water. Open holes with fingertips. Allow to dry in place. ❖

Beaded Beauty Set

Designs by Anne Bipes

Scarf

Skill Level

 ■■□□ EASY

Finished Size

5½ x 53 inches

Materials

- Bernat Softee Chunky (chunky weight; 100% acrylic; 180 yds/100g per ball): 2 balls buff #39018
- 25-inch length of scrap yarn
- Double-rake loom with at least 21 peg pairs
- Hook tool
- Size H/8 (5mm) crochet hook
- 576 beads, size 2/0
- Scissors
- Tapestry needle

Gauge

12½ stitches and 14 rows = 4 inches/10cm in Stockinette stitch.

Exact gauge is not critical to this project.

Instructions

Beaded Border

Step 1: Thread 288 beads onto each ball.

Step 2: Cast on 14 peg pairs, using peg pairs 2–15. There is one empty peg pair at the top, and two empty peg pairs at the bottom. Lay scrap yarn.

Step 3: Wrap loom for stockinette stitch, placing a bead against the groove in each peg on both sides of the loom. Knit off all pegs.

Step 4: Wrap loom, placing working yarn below the beads. Purl all pegs, placing beads on the inside of the loom against the back of the pegs.

Repeat [Steps 3 and 4] 8 more times—18 rows completed.

Body

Wrap and knit one row.

Add 1 stitch at each side of the knitting as follows: Move loops on pegs 2 to pegs 1, and move knit off loops on pegs 1 and 3 to empty pegs 2. Move loops on pegs 15 to pegs 16, and move knit off loops on pegs 14 and 16 to empty pegs 15.

Wrap, loom and knit all pegs until scarf is 45 inches long. On the first row, pegs 2 and 15 are knit off as two-over-one.

Decrease 1 stitch at each side of the knitting as follows: Move loops on pegs 2 to pegs 3, and move loops on pegs 1 to pegs 2. Move loops on pegs 15 to pegs 14, and move loops on pegs 16 to pegs 15.

Wrap loom and knit off; pegs 2 and 14 are knit off as two-over-one.

Beaded Border
Step 1: Wrap loom, placing working yarn below the beads. Purl all pegs, placing beads on the inside of the loom against the back of the pegs.

Step 2: Wrap loom for stockinette stitch, placing a bead against the groove in each peg on both sides of the loom. Knit off all pegs.

Step 3: Wrap loom, placing working yarn below the beads. Purl all pegs, placing beads on the inside of the loom against the back of the pegs.

Repeat [Steps 2 and 3] 8 more times—17 rows completed.

Bind off flat.

Finish cast on edge. Remove scrap yarn. Weave in tails.

Hat

Skill Level
◖■■■◗ INTERMEDIATE

Size
Woman's—one size fits most

Finished Size
19-inch diameter

Materials
• Bernat Softee Chunky (chunky weight; 100% acrylic; 180 yds/ 100g per ball): 1 ball buff #39018
• Two 30-inch lengths of scrap yarn
• Double-rake loom with at least 21 peg pairs
• Hook tool
• Size H/8 (5mm) crochet hook
• 210 beads, size 2/0
• Scissors
• Tapestry needle

Gauge

12½ stitches and 14 rows = 4 inches/10 cm in Stockinette stitch.

Exact gauge is not critical to project.

Instructions

Step 1: String 105 beads onto yarn.

Step 2: Cast on 21 peg pairs, lay scrap yarn.

Step 3: Wrap loom for stockinette stitch, placing a bead against the groove in each peg on one side of the loom only. Knit off all pegs.

Step 4: Wrap loom, placing working yarn below the beads on one side of the loom, and above the loops on the other side of the loom. Knit off the unbeaded side. Purl the beaded side, placing beads on the inside of the loom against the back of the pegs.

Repeat [Steps 3 and 4] 4 more times.

Knit 12 rows in stockinette stitch.

Decrease Row 1: Move loops on pegs 7 to pegs 6, and move remainder of loops over 1 peg so there are no empty pegs (i.e. pegs 8 to pegs 7, pegs 9 to pegs 8, etc.). Then move loops on pegs 13 to pegs 12 and move remainder of loops over 1 peg. Then move loops on pegs 19 to pegs 18. There will be loops on pegs 1–18 and two loops on pegs 6, 12 and 18. Wrap loom and knit off; pegs 6, 12, and 18 will be knit off as two-over-one.

Decrease Row 2: Move loops from pegs 6 to pegs 5, and then move remaining loops over one peg. Move loops from pegs 11 to pegs 10, and then move remaining loops. Move loops from pegs 16 to pegs 15. Wrap loom and knit off.

Decrease Row 3: Move loops from pegs 5 to pegs 4, and then move remaining loops. Move loops from pegs 9 to pegs 8, and then move remaining loops. Move loops from pegs 13 to pegs 12. Wrap loom and knit off.

Decrease Row 4: Move loops from pegs 4 to pegs 3, and then move remaining loops. Move loops from pegs 7 to pegs 6, and then move remaining loops. Move loops from pegs 10 to pegs 9. Wrap loom and knit off.

Decrease Row 5: Move loops from pegs 3 to pegs 2, and then move remaining loops. Move loops from pegs 5 to pegs 4, and then move remaining loops. Move loops from pegs 7 to pegs 6. Wrap loom and knit off.

Decrease Row 6: Move loops from pegs 2 to pegs 1, and then move remaining loops. Move loops from pegs 3 to pegs 2, and then move remaining loops. Move loops from pegs 4 to pegs 3. Wrap loom and knit off.

Bring loops from one side of the loom to the other side.

Cut yarn, leaving a 6-inch tail. Cut a 12-inch length of yarn and thread it into a tapestry needle. Thread through the loops on the pegs and remove knitting from the loom.

Repeat for second half of hat, *except* when removing knitting from the loom; use the same strand of yarn to thread through the loops, keeping the right (beaded) sides of the knit fabric together.

Finishing

Tie the yarn strands together tightly, gathering the top of the hat.

Turn the hat right side out, leaving the yarn tails on the inside.

Starting at the crown and working toward the brim, use a crochet slip stitch to make two side seams.

Finish the cast-on edges, completing the full circle. Remove scrap yarn.

Weave in tails on the inside of the hat.

Mittens

Skill Level

 ■■■□ INTERMEDIATE

Sizes

Woman's small/medium (large/extra-large)

Instructions are given for the smallest size, with larger size in parentheses. When only 1 number is given, it applies to all sizes.

Finished Sizes

4 x 10 (11) inches

Materials

- Bernat Softee Chunky (chunky weight; 100% acrylic; 180 yds/100g per ball): 1 ball buff #39018
- One 36-inch length and two 6-inch lengths of scrap yarn
- Double-rake loom with at least 18 peg pairs
- Hook tool
- Size H/8 (5mm) crochet hook
- 210 beads, size 2/0
- Scissors
- Tapestry needle

Gauge

12½ stitches and rows = 4 inches/10cm in Stockinette stitch.

Exact gauge is not critical to project.

Instructions

Cut a strand of yarn 20 (21) feet long and set aside for thumb.

Thread 105 beads onto the working yarn.

Cast on 15 peg pairs, using peg pairs 2 through 16. Leave one empty peg pair at the top and at least two empty peg pairs at the bottom. Lay scrap yarn.

Wrist

Row 1: Wrap loom for stockinette stitch, placing a bead against the groove in each peg on one side of the loom only. Knit off all pegs.

Row 2: Wrap loom, placing working yarn below the beads on one side of the loom, and above the loops on the other side of the loom. Knit off the unbeaded side. Purl the beaded side, placing beads on the inside of the loom against the back of the pegs.

Repeat [Rows 1 and 2] 4 more times—14 rows completed.

Wrap loom and knit all pegs.

Add stitches at pegs 3, 8 and 13, so 18 peg pairs are in use. Move loops to pegs as shown on Chart A.

From	To	From	To	From	To
2	1	16	17	17	18
3	2	15	16	16	17
Peg 3 is empty		14	15	15	16
		13	14	14	15
		12	13	Peg 14 is empty	
		11	12		
		10	11		
		9	10		
		Peg 9 is empty			

Move knit-off loops on pegs 2 and 4 to empty pegs 3, knit-off loops on pegs 8 and 10 to empty pegs 9, and knit-off loops on pegs 14 and 16 to empty pegs 15.

Knit 1 (4) rows. Pegs 3, 9 and 15 are knit off as two-over-one (on first row).

Thumb

Use pegs 6–9 for hand 1 and pegs 10–13 for hand 2. For hand 1, move knit-off loops on pegs 5 to pegs 6 and knit-off loops on pegs 10 to pegs 9. For hand 2, move knit-off loops on pegs 9 to pegs 10 and knit-off loops on pegs 14 to pegs 13.

With reserved yarn, on the 4 identified pegs only, knit 15 (17) rows. Cut remaining tail to 5 inches.

Hand

For hand 1, move knit-off loops on pegs 6 to pegs 5 and pegs 9 to pegs 10. For hand 2, move knit-off loops on pegs 10 to pegs 9 and pegs 13 to pegs 14.

With main strand of working yarn, using all pegs, knit 12 (14) rows.

Fingertips

Note: *Top and bottom halves of hand are worked separately, splitting between pegs 9 and 10.*

Move the loops on pegs 2 to pegs 3 and loops on pegs 1 to pegs 2. Wrap pegs 2–9 and knit off; peg 3 is knit off as two-over-one.

Move the loops on pegs 3 to peg 4 and pegs 2 to pegs 3. Wrap pegs 3–9 and knit off; pegs 4 are knit off as two-over-one.

Move the loops on pegs 4 to pegs 5, pegs 3 to pegs 4, pegs 8 to pegs 7 and pegs 9 to pegs 8. Wrap pegs 4–8 and knit off; pegs 5 and 7 are knit off as two-over-one.

Move the loops on pegs 5 to pegs 6, pegs 4 to pegs 5, pegs 7 to pegs 6 and pegs 8 to pegs 7. Wrap pegs 5–7 and knit off; pegs 6 are knit off as three-over-one.

Wrap and knit pegs 5–7 again. Cut yarn, leaving a 6-inch tail. Leave the 3 sets of loops on the loom.

Move the loops on pegs 17 to pegs 16 and loops on pegs 18 to pegs 17. Wrap pegs 10–17 and knit off; pegs 16 are knit off as two-over-one.

Move the loops on pegs 16 to pegs 15, and pegs 17 to pegs 16. Wrap pegs 10–16 and knit off; pegs 15 are knit off as two-over-one.

Move the loops on pegs 11 to pegs 12, pegs 10 to pegs 11, pegs 15 to pegs 14 and pegs 16 to pegs 15. Wrap pegs 11–15 and knit off; pegs 12 and 14 are knit off as two-over-one.

Move the loops on pegs 12 to pegs 13, pegs 11 to pegs 12, pegs 14 to pegs 13 and pegs 15 to pegs 14. Wrap pegs 12–14 and knit off; pegs 13 are knit off as three-over-one.

Wrap and knit pegs 12–14 again. Cut yarn, leaving a 6-inch tail.

Bring loops from one side of the loom to the other side for all 6 peg pairs in use. With a 6-inch length scrap yarn, thread yarn through loops 5–7. With another 6-inch length of scrap yarn, thread yarn through loops 1–14. Remove mitten from the loom.

Finishing

Fold mitten in half side to side, beaded side out. Starting at the top of the fold, use single crochet stitch to join front and back of mitten, working over the tops of the fingers and down to the cuff. When crocheting the live stitches at the top of the fingers, use the 4 live loops of each column of stitches together.

Starting at the top of the thumb fold and working toward the palm, use crochet slip stitch to close sides of thumb.

Loosely crochet slip stitch the live cast-on loops. Remove scrap yarn.

With a crochet hook, pull all tails to the inside of the mitten. Turn the mitten inside out and weave in the tails.

Repeat for the other hand. ❖

Arrowhead Double-Knit Scarf

Design by Anne Bipes

Skill Level

◼◼◼◻ INTERMEDIATE

Finished Size
4 x 58 inches

Materials

- Red Heart Soft Yarn (worsted weight; 100% acrylic; 256 yds/140g per skein): 1 skein each light grey heather #9440 (A) and mid blue #9820 (B)
- 20-inch length of scrap yarn
- Double-rake loom with at least 9 peg pairs
- Hook tool
- Size H/8 (5mm) crochet hook
- Scissors
- Tapestry needle

Gauge
9 stitches and 12 rows = 4 inches/10cm in Stockinette stitch.

Exact gauge is not critical to project.

Instructions
With A, cast on 9 peg pairs. Lay scrap yarn.

Note: Refer to Arrowhead chart and photos included to show color placement for row of wrap pattern.

House of White Birches, Berne, Indiana 46711

With both colors, follow
wrap pattern 1 and knit off.

With both colors, follow wrap
pattern 4 and knit off.

With both colors, follow wrap
pattern 2 and knit off.

With both colors, follow
wrap pattern 5 and knit off.

With both colors, follow
wrap pattern 3 and knit off.

With both colors, follow
wrap pattern 6 and knit off.

With both colors, follow wrap pattern 7 and knit off.

[Repeat last 9 rows] 8 more times.

With both colors, follow wrap pattern 1 and knit off.

With both colors, follow wrap pattern 2 and knit off.

With both colors, follow wrap pattern 3 and knit off.

With both colors, follow wrap pattern 4 and knit off.

With both colors, follow wrap pattern 5 and knit off.

With both colors, follow wrap pattern 6 and knit off.

With both colors, follow wrap pattern 7 and knit off.

With both colors, follow wrap pattern 10 and knit off.

With both colors, follow wrap pattern 11 and knit off.

With both colors, follow wrap pattern 8 and knit off.

With both colors, follow wrap pattern 9 and knit off.

With both colors, follow wrap pattern 12 and knit off.

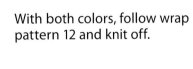

With both colors, follow wrap pattern 11 and knit off.

With both colors, follow wrap pattern 10 and knit off.

With both colors, follow wrap pattern 7 and knit off.

With both colors, follow wrap pattern 6 and knit off.

With both colors, follow wrap pattern 5 and knit off.

With both colors, follow wrap pattern 4 and knit off.

With both colors, follow wrap pattern 3 and knit off.

With both colors, follow wrap pattern 2 and knit off.

With both colors, follow wrap pattern 1 and knit off.

With both colors, follow wrap pattern 9 and knit off.

With both colors, follow wrap pattern 8 and knit off.

With both colors, follow wrap pattern 7 and knit off.

With both colors, follow wrap pattern 6 and knit off.

With both colors, follow wrap pattern 5 and knit off.

With both colors, follow wrap pattern 4 and knit off.

With both colors, follow wrap pattern 3 and knit off.

With both colors, follow wrap pattern 2 and knit off.

With both colors, follow wrap pattern 1 and knit off.

[Repeat last 9 rows] 8 more times.

Cut B, leaving a 6-inch tail.

Wrap loom with A for stockinette stitch and knit off.

Bring loops to one side and bind off.

Finish cast-on edge. Remove scrap yarn.

Weave in tails.

Finishing

For fringe, cut 18 strands 11 inches long of each color.

Using crochet hook and 1 strand of each color, place knot in each bound-off chain stitch on each end of the scarf. Trim ends even. ❖

COLOR KEY
■ Mid blue
□ Light grey heather

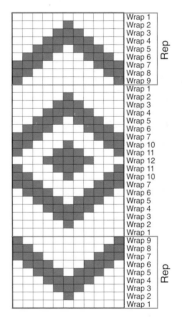

CHEVRON SCARF CHART
Chart shows how one side of the loom is wrapped; the other side of the loom has the opposite color.

Earth Mother's Slippers

Design by Anne Bipes

Skill Level
■■□□ EASY

Sizes
Youth (woman, man) Instructions are given for the smallest size, with larger sizes in parentheses. When only 1 number is given, it applies to all sizes.

Finished Measurements
4 (5, 6) x 7 (11, 15) inches, before felting

Materials

- Patons Classic Wool (worsted weight; 100% wool; 223 yds/100g per ball): 2 balls moss heather #77525
- 36-inch length of scrap yarn
- Double-rake loom with at least 20 (25, 29) peg pairs
- Hook tool
- Size H/8 (5mm) crochet hook
- 2 split-ring stitch markers
- Scissors
- Tapestry needle
- Lingerie bag or pillowcase
- Top-loading washing machine

Gauge
11 stitches and 14 rows = 4 inches/10cm in Stockinette stitch with 2 strands of yarn held together.

Exact gauge is not critical to this project.

Pattern Notes
Hold two strands of yarn together as one throughout unless instructed otherwise.

Use the stockinette stitch throughout.

Special Technique
To decrease 2 stitches at the end of the loom: Use the five loops at the end of the row; move loop 4 to peg 5, loop 3 to peg 4, loop 2 to peg 3, loop 1 to peg 2, then loop 3 to peg 4 and loop 2 to peg 3. When moves are complete, the end peg with have one loop, and the next two pegs will each have two loops. Wrap and knit row, bringing two loops over one for those pegs.

Instructions
Cast on 16 (21, 25) peg pairs, leaving at least 2 empty peg pairs at each end of the loom. Lay the scrap yarn between the rows of pegs.

Knit 14 (21, 25) rows in stockinette stitch.

Increase 2 stitches at each end of the loom. Place a stitch marker on one loop at each end of the loom.

Knit 12 (16, 25) rows.

Decrease 2 stitches at each end of the loom. Wrap and knit the row.

[Repeat the decrease row] 3 (5, 5) times. There are now 8 (5, 8) pegs in use.

Youth (man) sizes only: Decrease 1 stitch at each end of the loom, wrap and knit the row.

All sizes: Bring the loops from one side of the loom to the other. Cut 1 yarn strand to a 6-inch tail, and the other strand to a 20-inch tail. Thread the 20-inch tail into a tapestry needle and thread through the loops on the pegs. Remove knitting from the loom. Tie the tails tightly together, gathering the toe.

Use the long strand to whipstitch the top of the slipper closed, starting at the toe and ending at the stitch markers.

Close the back of the heel using a single crochet stitch, starting at the ankle and ending at the heel, catching four cast-on loops in each stitch.

Remove scrap yarn.

Weave in tails.

Make second slipper.

Felt as follows: Place slippers in a lingerie bag or pillowcase in a top-loading washing machine with a pair of jeans or tennis shoes. Start machine using the lowest water level, the hottest water, the

greatest agitation settings and no soap to felt slippers. Check slippers every few minutes for desired size; squeeze out extra moisture without twisting, or roll in a towel. Slippers will stretch a little while still wet. Put the slippers on to shape to your foot size. Allow to air dry, approximately 24 hours. ❖

Toasty-Toes Moccasins

Design by Anne Bipes

Skill Level

 INTERMEDIATE

Finished Size
Woman's medium

Finished Measurements
Foot length: 8 inches
Calf length: 8 inches

Materials
- Patons Shetland Chunky Tweeds (chunky weight; 72% acrylic/25% wool/3% viscose; 108 yds/85g per ball): 2 balls medium blue tweeds #67108
- 20-inch length of scrap yarn
- Double-rake loom with at least 10 peg pairs
- Hook tool
- Size H/8 (5mm) crochet hook
- Scissors
- Tapestry needle

5 BULKY

Gauge
9 stitches and 15 rows = 4 inches/10cm in Stockinette stitch.

Exact gauge is not critical to project.

Pattern Note
Sock is knit in stockinette stitch, with Double stockinette stitch used for the heel and sole to provide extra comfort and durability.

Special Techniques
To decrease with the double stockinette stitch:
On the second peg from the end, knit off the bottom loop over the top loop, leaving one loop on the loom. Move the remaining loop one peg over toward the center of the loom. Move the loops on the end peg over one peg toward the center of the loom. After wrapping the loom, knit of the second to last peg as two loops over two loops.

To increase with the stockinette stitch: Move the loops on the end pegs away from the knitting by one peg. Pick up the just-knit-off loop from the second peg and put it on the empty peg.

Instructions

Back of leg
Cast on 10 peg pairs, lay scrap yarn.

Knit 24 rows in stockinette stitch.

Heel & Sole
Wrap loom twice so there are three loops on each peg; knit off by bringing the bottom loop over the top 2 loops and off the peg.

Knit 42 rows with double stockinette stitch.

Toe
Next row: Decrease 1 stitch at end of row, wrap loom and knit off.

Next row: Knit.

[Repeat last two rows] 4 more times. 5 peg pairs are now in use.

Knit 4 rows.

Without wrapping the loom, knit 1 row, leaving one loop on each peg.

Knit two rows in stockinette stitch.

Next row: Increase 1 stitch at end of row, wrap loom and knit off.

Next row: Knit.

[Repeat last 2 rows] 4 more times. 10 peg pairs are now in use.

Top of foot & front of leg
Knit 37 rows.

Bring loops to one side in preparation for bind off.

Thread a piece of scrap yarn into a tapestry needle, thread needle through all loops and remove knitting from the loom.

Finishing

Sew heel
Count 8 rows from the start of the double stockinette and fold heel. On the outside of the sock, slip stitch crochet the side of the heel with

5 stitches, catching the loops of every other knit stitch.

Repeat for other side of heel.

Sew sides
Fold the slipper sock at the toe where the double stockinette stitch ends and the stockinette stitch begins.

On the outside of the sock, starting at the toe, slip stitch crochet both sides.

Join top
Finish the entire edge of the sock with the crochet slip stitch.

Remove scrap yarn.

On inside, weave in tails.

Repeat for other sock, folding the knitting at the heel and toe in the other direction for the other foot. ❖

Woodsy-Warmth Shawl

Continued from page 25

Finish cast-on edge. Remove scrap yarn.

Weave in tails.

Fringe
Cut 60 strands each 11 inches long.

With crochet hook, attach one strand to each bound-off chain stitch on each end of the shawl.

Trim ends even. ❖

Meet the Designer

Anne Bipes has been knitting with looms since 2004, when her daughter was intimidated by the double-point needles used for the hat she wanted to make. She began to design new patterns for loom knitting and has shared her expertise with others in person, in print and via the Web. She lives in Minnesota with her husband and daughter.

Knitting Needle Conversion Chart

U.S.	1	2	3	4	5	6	7	8	9	10	10½	11	13	15	17	19	35	50
Continental-mm	2.25	2.75	3.25	3.5	3.75	4	4.5	5	5.5	6	6.5	8	9	10	12	15	19	25

Inches into Millimetres & Centimetres

All measurements are rounded off slightly.

inches	mm	cm	inches	cm	inches	cm	inches	cm	inches	cm
⅛	3	0.3	3	7.5	13	33.0	26	66.0	39	99.0
¼	6	0.6	3½	9.0	14	35.5	27	68.5	40	101.5
⅜	10	1.0	4	10.0	15	38.0	28	71.0	41	104.0
½	13	1.3	4½	11.5	16	40.5	29	73.5	42	106.5
⅝	15	1.5	5	12.5	17	43.0	30	76.0	43	109.0
¾	20	2.0	5½	14	18	46.0	31	79.0	44	112.0
⅞	22	2.2	6	15.0	19	48.5	32	81.5	45	114.5
1	25	2.5	7	18.0	20	51.0	33	84.0	46	117.0
1¼	32	3.8	8	20.5	21	53.5	34	86.5	47	119.5
1½	38	3.8	9	23.0	22	56.0	35	89.0	48	122.0
1¾	45	4.5	10	25.5	23	58.5	36	91.5	49	124.5
2	50	5.0	11	28.0	24	61.0	37	94.0	50	127.0
2½	65	6.5	12	30.5	25	63.5	38	96.5		

Skill Levels

BEGINNER

Beginner projects for first-time knitters using basic stitches. Minimal shaping.

EASY

Easy projects using basic stitches, repetitive stitch patterns, simple color changes, and simple shaping and finishing.

INTERMEDIATE

Intermediate projects using a variety of stitches, mid-level shaping and finishing.

EXPERIENCED

Experienced projects using advanced techniques and stitches, detailed shaping and refined finishing.

HOUSE of WHITE BIRCHES
PUBLISHERS SINCE 1947

Learn to Knit on Long Looms is published by DRG, 306 East Parr Road, Berne, IN 46711. Printed in USA. Copyright © 2010 DRG. All rights reserved. This publication may not be reproduced in part or in whole without written permission from the publisher.

RETAIL STORES: If you would like to carry this pattern book or any other DRG publications, visit DRGwholesale.com

Every effort has been made to ensure that the instructions in this publication are complete and accurate. We cannot, however, take responsibility for human error, typographical mistakes or variations in individual work. Please visit AnniesCustomerCare.com to check for pattern updates.

STAFF

Editor: Barb Bettegnies
Assistant Editor: Stephanie Timm
Technical Editor: Kathy Wesley
Technical Artist: Pam Gregory
Copy Supervisor: Michelle Beck
Copy Editors: Emily Carter, Amanda Scheerer
Production Artist Supervisor: Erin Augsburger

Graphic Artists: Debby Keel, Amanda Treharn
Art Director: Brad Snow
Assistant Art Director: Nick Pierce
Photography Supervisor: Tammy Christian
Photography: Matthew Owen
Photo Stylists: Tammy Leichty, Tammy Steiner

ISBN: 978-1-59217-295-5

4 5 6 7 8 9

Photo Index

14

16

32

18

25

26

21

42

22

28

44

37